INTERFACT ™

THE BOOK AND DISK THAT WORK TOGETHER

SOLAR SYSTEM

TWO CAN ™

PRINCETON ▪ LONDON

Book and disk by
act-two Ltd

Published in the United States and Canada by
Two-Can Publishing LLC
234 Nassau Street
Princeton, NJ 08542

This edition Copyright © 2000 Two-Can Publishing LLC

For information on other Two-Can books and multimedia,
Call 1-609-921-6700, fax 1-609-921-3349, or visit our web site at
http://www.two-canpublishing.com

ISBN: 1-58728-464-2

2 4 6 8 10 9 7 5 3

Photographic Credits: front cover tbc
pp.6–7 NASA pp.10–11 NASA/Starland Picture LIbrary p.13 NASA p.14 NASA p.15 NASA p.17
(top right) NASA/Starland Picture Library (left) Ian Graham p.18 NASA pp.18–19 Julian Baum p.19
NASA p.20 Julian Baum p.21 NASA pp.22–23 Julian Baum p.23 (top left) NASA (top right) NASA p.24
Julian Baum p.25 US Naval Observatory p.26 Ian Graham p.34 NASA p.35 NASA/Ian Graham
Illustration Credits: All illustrations by Chris Forsey and Peter Bull except those
on pages. 28–32, which are by Graham Humphries of Virgil Pomfret Artists

Printed in Hong Kong by Wing King Tong

INTERFACT will have you hooked in minutes –
and that's a fact!

⬤ **The disk is full of interactive activities, puzzles, quizzes, and games that are fun to do and packed with interesting facts.**

Save Alan the Astronaut with your space knowledge by playing Lost in Space.

Click to continue.

⬤ **Open the book and discover more fascinating information highlighted with lots of full-color illustrations and photographs.**

The sun

The sun is a star. Compared to many other stars, it is quite ordinary. Other stars may be bigger or smaller, hotter or colder than the sun. From our viewpoint, the sun seems to be the biggest star of all, but this is only because it is the nearest star to Earth.

The sun is a huge ball of gases, mainly hydrogen and helium. At its center, the temperature and pressure are so great that hydrogen **atoms** are forced together to form helium atoms by a process called thermonuclear fusion. When they do this, they release a huge amount of **energy** in the form of heat and light. Earth receives a tiny fraction of the sun's total energy output, but it is enough to warm Earth and to provide the light that makes life possible.

SUN FACTS
● The sun is about 870,000 miles (1.4 million km) across. It is 27 million °F (15 million °C) at its core.

DISK LINK
The sun is divided into six layers. To learn more about the sun's layers, play Rocket Mission.

The sun's core

◀ Explosions on the sun's surface can release gas in an arch called a prominence. Solar flares send out high-speed particles that can interfere with radio signals on Earth.

▶ The corona, the sun's outermost layer, extends millions of miles or kilometers into space. It is visible during a solar eclipse, which occurs when the moon passes between Earth and the sun.

How does the sun create so much energy? Read up and find out!

⬤ To get the most out of **INTERFACT,** use the book and disk together. Look for the special signs called Disk Links and Bookmarks. To find out more, turn to page 43.

23

BOOKMARK

DISK LINK
Look at a comet close up when you play Here Comes The Comet!

Once you've launched **INTERFACT,** you'll never look back.

LOAD UP!
Go to **page 40** to find out how to load your disks and click into action.

What's on the disk

HELP SCREEN

Learn how to use the disk in no time at all.

These are the controls the Help Screen will tell you how to use:
- arrow keys
- reading boxes
- "hot" words

ROCKET MISSION

Are you ready for a journey into the depths of space?

Take command of a spacecraft and blast into space on a voyage of cosmic discovery. The solar system is yours! Visit any planet you choose and then learn all about it.

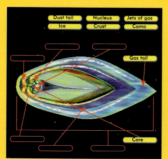

HERE COMES THE COMET

Examine a comet close up.

Why does a comet burn and what have people thought of them in the past? Try to label the comet correctly and you can find out.

LOST IN SPACE

Have you got what it takes to be a galactic whiz kid?

Test your brain power with this quiz on the solar system and its amazing objects. Just click to join in. It's out of this world!

SHUTTLE SECRETS

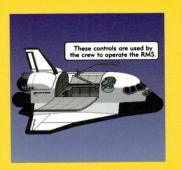

These controls are used by the crew to operate the RMS.

Here's your chance to explore an interactive space shuttle!

What makes the space shuttle so special? How is it different from other spacecraft? Explore the interactive space shuttle with your mouse and discover how its parts work.

OUT OF THIS WORLD

What are asteroids?

Get the answers to some cosmic questions!

Do you know how big the solar system is? Eva will ask RAD the questions that you want answers to. Get the lowdown on meteors, asteroids, galaxies, and the sun!

TIME LINE

The United States launched the Hubble Space telescope in 1990. Hubble has been used to find evidence for black holes.

FUTURE PAST

Go back in time and delve into the history of astronomy and space travel!

Watch Astro get older or younger as you slide him along the Time Line. See how our understanding of the universe has changed throughout history.

METEOR MADNESS

Are you the one to save Earth from destruction?

Save Earth from a storm of meteorites by answering the questions correctly. Your knowledge could make you the hero of the world!

What's in the book

*All words in the text that appear in **bold** can be found in the glossary*

Our solar system

Our solar system is made up of the sun and everything that is affected by the sun's **gravitation**. The planets, the **moons** that circle the planets, and a variety of other objects, including **comets**, move the way they do because of the sun's gravitational attraction.

There are nine planets. Our planet, Earth, is the third from the sun. The planets are all quite different. Many of these differences result from their different distances from the sun.

We call the planets that are closer to the sun, including Earth, the inner planets. They are small, rocky worlds. The outer planets are much larger and are made from much lighter materials. At least one moon orbits each of the planets except two – Mercury and Venus.

▼ The sun and the objects held by its gravitation make up the solar system. The sun contains more than 99 percent of the mass, or material, of our solar system.

1. Mercury
2. Venus
3. Earth
4. Mars
5. Jupiter
6. Sun
7. Saturn
8. Uranus
9. Neptune
10. Pluto

SOLAR SYSTEM FACTS

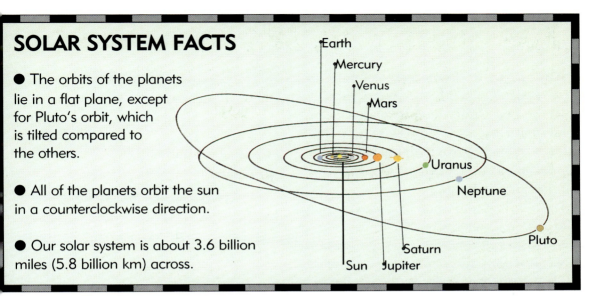

● The orbits of the planets lie in a flat plane, except for Pluto's orbit, which is tilted compared to the others.

● All of the planets orbit the sun in a counterclockwise direction.

● Our solar system is about 3.6 billion miles (5.8 billion km) across.

DISK LINK
Our solar system is part of a galaxy. To find out more about galaxies, ask RAD in Out of This World.

The sun

The sun is a star. Compared to many other stars, it is quite ordinary. Other stars may be bigger or smaller, hotter or colder than the sun. From our viewpoint, the sun seems to be the biggest star of all, but this is only because it is the nearest star to Earth.

The sun is a huge ball of gases, mainly hydrogen and helium. At its center, the temperature and pressure are so great that hydrogen **atoms** are forced together to form helium atoms by a process called thermonuclear fusion. When they do this, they release a huge amount of **energy** in the form of heat and light. Earth receives a tiny fraction of the sun's total energy output, but it is enough to warm Earth and to provide the light that makes life possible.

SUN FACTS

- The sun is about 870,000 miles (1.4 million km) across. It is 27 million °F. (15 million °C) at its core.

DISK LINK
The sun is divided into six layers. To learn more about the sun's layers, play Rocket Mission.

The sun's core

◄ Explosions on the sun's surface can release gas in an arch called a prominence. Solar flares send out high-speed particles that interfere with radio signals on Earth.

► The corona, the sun's outermost layer, extends millions of miles or kilomete into space. It is visible durir a solar eclipse, which occu when the moon passes between Earth and the sur

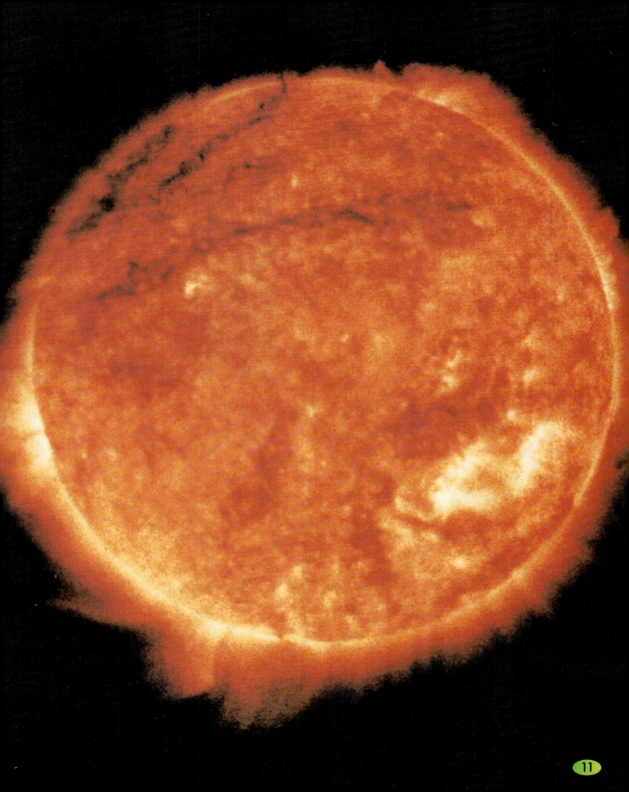

Earth and the moon

Our home planet of Earth is, as far as we know, the only planet in our solar system where life has evolved. It is also the only planet in our solar system with flowing water on its surface. Almost three-quarters of Earth's surface is covered by water.

The pull of Earth's gravity traps a layer of air, called the **atmosphere,** around it. Earth's rocky surface, or crust, is not as solid and stationary as it seems. It consists of a number of separate plates that move. Where they meet, they rub against each other. This is what causes **earthquakes** and **volcanoes.** Earth's surface is also changed by the action of wind, rain, and tides.

▲ The moon's force of gravity is only one sixth of Earth's. As a result, the moon is unable to hold an atmosphere.

EARTH FACTS

● Earth's core is made of iron, with a solid center and a liquid outer core. Around this is a layer of melted rock called the mantle. On the outside is the crust, a thin layer of rock.

● The layer of gases that lies between Earth and outer space is called the atmosphere.

● Earth formed from material orbiting the sun about 4.5 billion years ago.

MOON FACTS

● The moon is the only other place in the solar system apart from Earth where human beings have set foot. Between 1969 and 1972, a total of 12 astronauts landed on the moon.

DISK LINK
What was said by the first astronaut as he set foot on the moon? Find out in Time Line.

PAST

The tides – the twice-daily rise and fall in sea level – are caused by the moon. As the moon orbits Earth, the moon's gravitational force pulls the water away from the solid Earth, raising the water level.

▲ Earth's blue oceans, brown land masses, and white clouds make it one of the most colorful planets in our solar system. This photograph was taken from space by a weather satellite orbiting Earth at a height of 22,000 miles (36,000 km).

Mercury and Venus

Mercury is the closest planet to the sun. It is so close that in Mercury's sky the sun is two-and-a-half times bigger than it is in Earth's sky. The side of Mercury that faces the sun is heated to 800° F. (430° C), which is hot enough to melt lead. As the planet turns away from the sun, the nighttime temperature plunges to −270 °F. (−170° C).

When the U.S. space probe Mariner 10 flew past Mercury in 1974–1975, it sent back pictures of a rocky planet, a third of the size of Earth and covered with craters that looked like those on the moon.

Venus is nearly the same size as Earth, but it is a very different world. Its atmosphere contains mainly carbon dioxide, and its clouds are full of droplets of sulfuric acid. The pressure at its surface is about 90 times the pressure at Earth's surface.

DISK LINK
Venus may once have had oceans that have since dried up. This fact may help when you're Lost in Space!

◀ This picture of Mercury was taken by Mariner 10 in March 1974. It shows Mercury's heavily cratered surface.

▶ This photograph of Venus shows the planet's thick covering of clouds. The U.S. Pioneer probe used **radar** to look through the cloud and see the surface.

VENUS FACTS

● Russian space probes have taken pictures of Venus's rocky surface. Its sky is orange-yellow.

● Venus is the second brightest object in the night sky, after the moon.

Mars

The planet Mars has fascinated people for thousands of years. We have evidence to prove that some ancient civilizations worshiped it as a god. Mars was the Roman god of war. In 1877, an Italian astronomer named Giovanni Schiaparelli drew a map of Mars. It caused a great stir because the planet was shown criss-crossed with what Schiaparelli described as channels.

When Schiaparelli's work was published in English, the word *channels* was translated as *canals.* This led some scientists to believe that they were made by intelligent beings. For the next 70 years, scientists disagreed about whether there was intelligent life on Mars. In the 1970's, the Viking space probes visited Mars. As a result, people finally discovered that Mars has no canals or intelligent creatures.

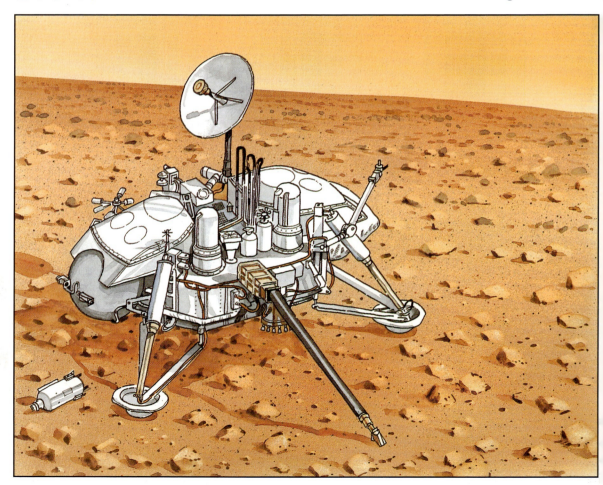

This photograph of Mars taken from Earth shows one of its polar ice caps, but little else. More detailed studies of Mars were made possible by space probes.

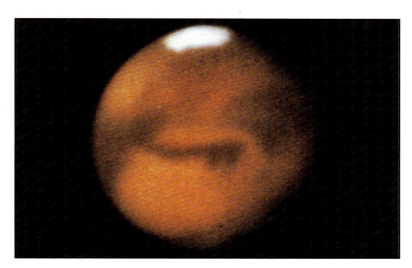

▼ Mars, also called the Red Planet, has a huge volcano called Olympus Mons. It is 15 miles (25 km) high and 370 miles (600 km) across.

MARS FACTS

● Mars's **diameter** is half of Earth's. Its force of gravity is weaker. If you weighed 110 pounds (50 kg) on Earth, you would weigh only 42 pounds (19 kg) on Mars.

● A Martian day is only a few minutes longer than an Earth-day, but the Martian year is 687 Earth-days.

● Mars looks like a red star in the sky. It is brightest every 780 days, when it is on the opposite side of the sun from Earth. Mars has two moons, called Phobos and Deimos.

DISK LINK
How hot is the surface of Mars? Find out when you play Rocket Mission.

◀ A U.S. Viking lander sits on Mars just as two Viking spacecraft did in 1976. Each one took photographs around its landing site and tested the soil for signs of life.

Jupiter

Jupiter is the giant of our solar system's nine planets. About 1,000 Earths would fit inside it. Jupiter is unlike any of the rocky inner planets, including Earth. It is a huge ball of gas and liquid, perhaps with a small rocky core. It is made mostly of hydrogen and helium, just like a star. In fact, Jupiter seems to be a star that failed to "light up." It was unable to attract enough material to create the high temperature and pressure at its core that are necessary for nuclear fusion to begin.

Jupiter's most obvious feature is its Great Red Spot. This feature is actually a storm that has been raging in Jupiter's atmosphere for at least as long as people have been observing the planet – and that's more than 300 years!

▼ Until U.S. space probes flew past the outer planets, only Saturn was known to be encircled by rings. Then the Voyager spacecraft also discovered rings around Uranus, Neptune, and Jupiter (below).

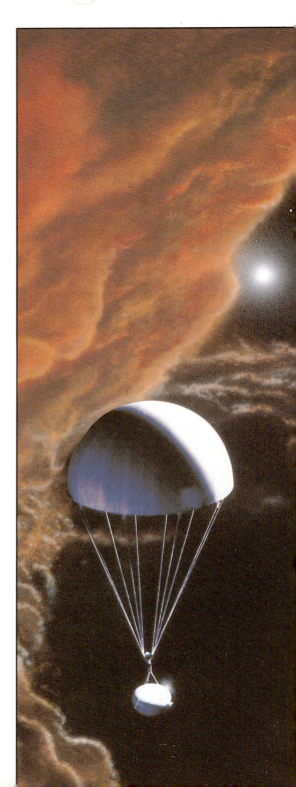

DISK LINK
Who discovered moons around Jupiter in 1610? Find out in Time Line.

PAST

JUPITER FACTS

● Jupiter is bigger and heavier than all the other planets combined.

● Jupiter has 16 known moons. Liquid water was discovered on one in 1997.

Earth

● Jupiter rotates rapidly. This planet takes less than 10 hours to rotate once.

◀ A probe plunges into Jupiter's clouds.

▼ The Great Red Spot is always changing. Three cloud systems formed in 1940. One is visible below the Great Red Spot.

Saturn

Saturn, with its flattened disk of rings, is a most spectacular sight. The rings change in appearance depending on whether they are tilted toward Earth or have their edges facing Earth. When viewed edge-on, they seem to disappear.

Saturn is the second biggest planet in the solar system. Like Jupiter, it is mostly liquid hydrogen. It has at least 18 moons. The largest, Titan, has a thick atmosphere of nitrogen gas.

▶ This image shows Saturn and its largest moons, compiled from Voyager photos. The probe showed that the broad rings were actually hundreds of narrow ringlets.

SATURN FACTS

● Saturn is nearly 10 times as far from the sun as Earth, so it is much colder. It receives only one-hundredth as much heat from the sun as Earth does.

● Saturn is about 75,000 miles (120,000 km) across. That is almost 10 times the diameter of Earth.

Earth

▲ Some of Saturn's ringlets are held in place by the gravity of nearby moons, or shepherd satellites. The intertwining of some rings is believed to be caused by these satellites.

DISK LINK
If you want to save Earth in Meteor Madness, remember what you read!

Uranus, Neptune, and Plu

Each of the outer planets – Uranus, Neptune, and Pluto – is strange in its own way. Uranus' axis is so tilted that it lies on its side, with one pole and then the other facing the sun.

Neptune has a dark region called the Great Dark Spot—a swirling, hurricane-like mass of gas that resembles Jupiter's Great Red Spot.

Pluto's orbit may be its most unusual feature. It travels around the sun in a different plane than the other planets, and it also sometimes crosses inside Neptune's orbit. Pluto also has a moon, Charon, that is more than one-half the size of Pluto. To compare, Earth's moon only about one-fourth the size of Earth.

▼ Voyager 2 passed within 66,000 miles (107,000 km) of Uranus.

▼ By photographing Neptune through filters, Voyager measured the amount of methane gas in its atmosphere.

▲ An artist created this painting of Pluto; its moon, Charon; and the distant sun.

COLD FACTS

● Uranus and Neptune each consist of a ball of hydrogen and helium gases, with a rocky core surrounded by ice. They are almost the same size, roughly 30,000 miles (49,000 km) in diameter.

● With a diameter of 1,430 miles (2,300 km), Pluto is the smallest planet.

DISK LINK
You can visit all three of these planets when you take part in Rocket Mission!

Comets, asteroids, and meteorites

A broad band of rocky chunks called asteroids lies in the asteroid belt, between the orbits of Mars and Jupiter. The largest asteroids are also called minor planets. One theory is that they are the parts of a planet that failed to come together.

▼ During the 1990's, the Galileo space probe orbited Jupiter to study the planet. It is shown here passing an asteroid.

DID YOU KNOW?

● Not all asteroids are located in the asteroid belt. Three groups of asteroids, called the Atens, the Amors, and the Apollos, orbit near the inner planets. Several have passed fairly close to Earth. The Trojan asteroids follow the same orbit as Jupiter.

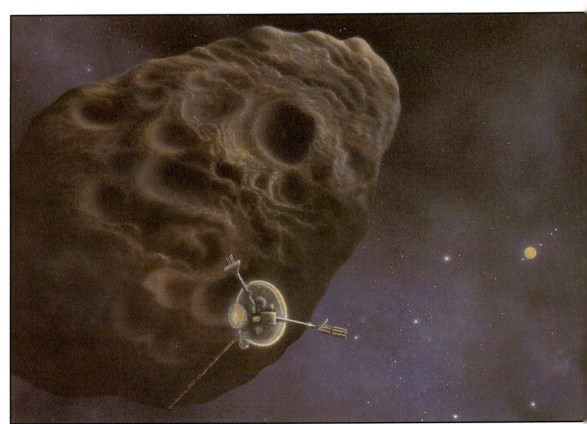

Comets and meteors often can be seen from Earth. Comets are balls of dirty ice that orbit the sun. The head of a comet is called the nucleus. Gas evaporating from the nucleus forms a cloud, called the coma. The solar wind — particles that fly away from the sun — blows the tail away from the sun.

A meteor is a streak of light that is seen in the night sky for a moment and then disappears. Meteors are produced when small pieces of rock enter Earth's atmosphere and burn up.

▼ Comet Ikeya-Seki was visible in 1975. The nucleus and coma can be seen clearly.

DISK LINK
What's the difference between a meteor and a meteorite? RAD has the answer in Out of This World.

Space probe

Unmanned space probes, such as the Pioneer and Voyager spacecraft, have explored vast expanses of our solar system. They have sent back photographs and information by radio, from hundreds of millions of miles or kilometers away.

We know a great deal more about the sun, the planets, their moons, and even the origin of our solar system thanks to deep space probes. The two Voyager space probes sent back more than 30,000 photographs from Jupiter alone.

They then went on to visit most of the outer planets.

DISK LINK
What is a space shuttle, and how does it work? Find out with the help of Shuttle Secrets!

▼ A space probe nears Saturn. Its dish aerial receives commands and sends information back to Earth.

MAKE A MODEL OF A SPACE PROBE

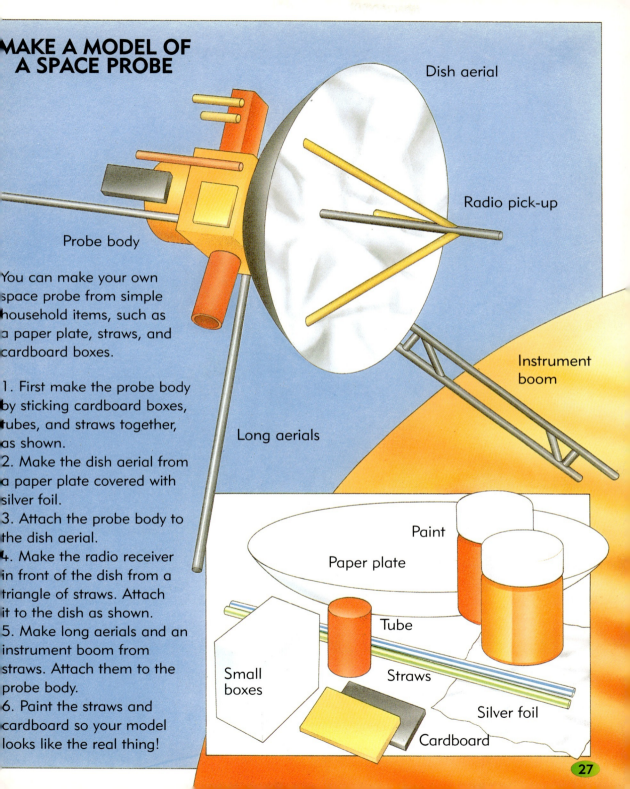

Dish aerial

Radio pick-up

Probe body

You can make your own space probe from simple household items, such as a paper plate, straws, and cardboard boxes.

1. First make the probe body by sticking cardboard boxes, tubes, and straws together, as shown.
2. Make the dish aerial from a paper plate covered with silver foil.
3. Attach the probe body to the dish aerial.
4. Make the radio receiver in front of the dish from a triangle of straws. Attach it to the dish as shown.
5. Make long aerials and an instrument boom from straws. Attach them to the probe body.
6. Paint the straws and cardboard so your model looks like the real thing!

Long aerials

Instrument boom

Paint

Paper plate

Tube

Small boxes

Straws

Silver foil

Cardboard

A journey through our solar system

Ever since more powerful modern rockets began to be developed in the 1950's, people have imagined journeys to distant planets and beyond. This description of an imaginary journey into space is set in the year 2050, when it is expected that space travel will be quite commonplace.

"Crossing Saturn's orbit," the ship's electronic voice purrs from the speaker in the corner of the cabin. Most of the passengers go to the windows, hoping to catch a glimpse of the ringed planet. The passengers are all science officers who are returning to Earth after a five-year tour of duty at the space station Deep Space Observatory. DSO is in permanent orbit around the planet Neptune.

The scientists travel in the ferrycraft Solar Explorer 2. The spacecraft's engines work by heating liquid hydrogen in a nuclear reactor. The engines provide the initial acceleration to move the craft out of Neptune's orbit and to make course corrections. But for most of the journey, the craft "coasts" unpowered. It uses the pull of gravity of the various planets to help to bring it back to Earth.

Hydrogen-powered turbines generate the craft's electricity. Closer to the sun, solar panels can be used. But in the outer reaches of the solar system, there is not enough light for them to work efficiently.

The cylindrical middle section of the 90-foot (150-meter) long spacecraft spins just fast enough to produce a force against its outer wall similar to Earth's gravity. To the people on board this section, "up" is toward the center of the spacecraft. However, the flight deck, where the commander, engineering officer, and pilot work, does not spin. Because these crew members are weightless, they must be strapped into their seats while they work. This prevents any unecessary accidents while they float around the deck.

"Over here," someone calls out. The passengers all gather at the windows. In the far distance, Saturn lies like a glowing, golden ball on a black velvet sheet. Its flattened disk of rings is tipped toward the spacecraft, showing off the rings at their best. The spacecraft's forward video camera slowly rotates to point at the planet. The screen shows hundreds of bright rings packed closely together. The rings seem to shine and sparkle in the darkness.

"We won't be so lucky with Jupiter," says one of the crew. "By the time we reach Jupiter's orbit, the planet will be hundreds of millions of kilometers away on the other side of the sun."

"It's going to be a long trip then," says a passenger.

The crew member nods. "But Jupiter is so massive that the extra acceleration from its gravitational field can make all the difference between a short and a long voyage."

Saturn disappears from the viewing screen, and one of several safety and training films, shown to every group of passengers, begins. The passengers return to their seats and the presenter explains the next stage of the flight.

"Soon we will begin reducing speed to prepare for the asteroid belt." This is a region of space between the orbits of Mars and Jupiter, where countless millions of rocks orbit the sun. It is a very dangerous area for any spacecraft. "In three hours we will make a course correction that will pitch us up over the densest region of the belt," the presenter continues. "We will maintain our reduced speed until the positions and trajectories of all large objects in our vicinity are mapped. We will then be able to enter the asteroid field at the safest moment."

During an average journey through the asteroid belt, perhaps more than two dozen large chunks of rock come within sight of the spacecraft. These and many smaller objects are tracked by using radar to ensure that none of them endanger the spacecraft.

The viewing screen begins to show a film of a spacecraft on a previous flight as it journeys through the asteroid belt. Large rocky objects—the asteroids—glide across the screen. Some are as big as small planets. A smallish gray spacecraft is highlighted against the yellow background of one of the larger asteroids.

"That's a miner," says one of the scientists. Asteroids rich in valuable minerals are mined by a fleet of mining craft. These operate from mother ships lying in safer space outside the asteroid belt. Once safely through the belt, Solar Explorer 2 sets a course for Mars.

On such a long journey, passengers without specific jobs to do often become very bored. There is nothing to see through the observation windows apart from the occasional close approach to a planet. For most of the journey, there is nothing but darkness and stars outside.

Radio messages take so long to travel from Earth to the craft that two-way conversations are impossible. Most passengers record messages to be transmitted to Earth and then read, play games, or watch video films while they wait for replies.

To make the journey pass more quickly, passengers can apply for a sleep pattern regulation program. By wearing a cap fitted with electrodes, the passenger's brain waves can be modified to make him or her sleep longer – up to several days at a time – with no ill effects.

Soon after crossing the orbit of Mars, sleep pattern regulation is brought to an end. This is done to give passengers plenty of time to adjust to normal day and night cycles before they arrive back on Earth. At its closest approach to Mars, Earth is only 35 million miles (56 million km) away. The journey is nearing its end.

In common with all interplanetary spacecraft, the Solar Explorer will not land on Earth. It was not designed to withstand the high temperatures, forces, and friction normally experienced by a spacecraft entering a planet's atmosphere. Instead, it will dock with a space station that permanently orbits Earth. For the last stage of the journey home, the passengers will transfer to a shuttle craft, which is more resistant to heat and pressure.

Excitement quickly grows among the passengers as Earth comes into view and two-way radio conversations become possible. The Solar Explorer has visited many strange worlds. And the passengers will never forget the amazing things they saw. But the other planets of the solar system are either violently stormy, hostile worlds or dead chunks of cratered rock. Compared to them, the bright sphere of the temperate Earth, covered by curling white swirls of cloud and deep blue oceans, looks very welcoming.

True or false?

Which of these facts are true and which are false? If you have read this book carefully, you will know the answers!

1. Our solar system consists of the sun, the planets, their moons, and all objects trapped by the sun's gravity.

2. The inner planets, the four planets that are closest to the sun, are all small, rocky worlds.

3. Jupiter is so big that it contains more material than all the planets combined.

4. Arches of gas thrown out from the sun's surface are called prominences.

5. The sun is made up of a wide variety of gases, but it consists mostly of carbon dioxide and oxygen.

6. The moon has an atmosphere of various kinds of gases.

7. Saturn's famous rings are solid disks of frozen hydrogen and ice mixed with particles of dust blown by winds.

8. Tides are caused by the solar wind blowing water against the shore.

9. Most asteroids lie between the orbits of Mars and Jupiter.

Glossary

Atmosphere is a layer of gas that surrounds some stars, planets, and moons. The Earth's atmosphere is about four-fifths nitrogen and one-fifth oxygen, with tiny amounts of a few other gases. Other planets have different atmospheres.

Atoms are the smallest units of any material that can take part in chemical reactions.

Comet is a small ball of dirty ice that orbits the sun. As it approaches the sun and is heated by it, gases evaporate from it and form a long tail. Comet Hale-Bopp was clearly visible from Earth in 1997.

Diameter is the width of a circle or sphere (ball). Planets are not perfect spheres – their diameters are measured across their equators.

Earthquakes are violent shakings of the Earth's surface. They are caused by brittle rocks in the Earth's crust breaking up as plates in the crust rub and move against each other.

Energy enables living creatures to survive. There are many different forms of energy, including heat, light, sound, and electrical and chemical energy.

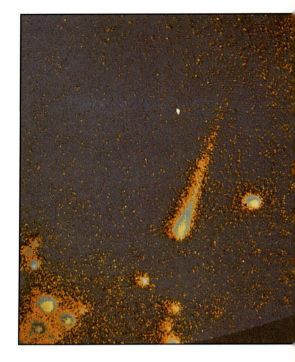

▲ Skylab took this photo of Comet Kohoutek (center) high above the Earth's atmosphere on Christmas Day, 1973.

Equator is an imaginary line around a planet, midway between its north and south poles.

Gravitation, or gravity, is a force that attracts objects to each other. It pulls things on Earth down toward the center of the Earth. The more massive the object, the greater its gravitational force.

Magnetic field is a region of space where the effect of a magnet exists.

Milky Way is the star system, or galaxy, to which our solar system belongs.

▲ Four of Saturn's moons orbit the planet. This scene was compiled from Voyager I spacecraft photographs.

Moons are the natural objects that orbit a planet.

Radar is a system used to detect and locate objects that are either hidden or are too far away to be seen.

Volcanoes are holes in a planet's crust where molten rock may spew out.

SOLAR SYSTEM FACTS

● Our solar system formed from a swirling cloud of dust and gas in one of the arms of a spiral galaxy called the **Milky Way** about 4.6 billion years ago.

● Neptune's largest moon, Triton, is falling toward Neptune. In 10 million to 100 million years, Triton will collide with the planet.

● The planet with the strongest gravitation is, not surprisingly, the largest – Jupiter. The gravitational force at Jupiter's surface is 2.64 times that of Earth. Someone who weighs 10 pounds (50 kg) on Earth would weigh 290 pounds (130 kg) on Jupiter.

● The closest star to the sun is Proxima Centauri, a small, cool type of star called a red dwarf. Traveling at the speed of light, it would take 4.3 years to reach Proxima Centauri.

● The closer a planet is to the sun, the shorter its year. Mercury's year is 88 Earth-days long. Pluto's is 248 Earth-years long. Earth, which lies between the two, has 365.25 days in a year.

● The Voyager spacecraft discovered that, in addition to Saturn, whose rings had already been seen from Earth, Jupiter, Uranus, and Neptune also are encircled by rings.

Lab pages

Photocopy these sheets and use them to make your own notes.

Lab pages

Photocopy these sheets and use them to make your own notes.

Loading your INTERFACT disk

INTERFACT is easy to load. But, before you begin, quickly run through the checklist on the opposite page to ensure that your computer is ready to run the program.

Your INTERFACT CD-ROM will run on both PCs with Windows and on Apple Macs. To make sure that your computer meets the system requirements, check the list below.

SYSTEM REQUIREMENTS

PC
- 486DX2/66 Mhz Processor
- Windows 3.1, 3.11, 95, 98 (or later)
- 8 Mb RAM (16 Mb recommended for Windows 95 and 24 Mb recommended for Windows 98)
- VGA colour monitor
- SoundBlaster-compatible soundcard

APPLE MACINTOSH
- 68020 processor
- system 7.0 (or later)
- 16 Mb of RAM

LOADING INSTRUCTIONS

You can run INTERFACT from the disk – you don't need to install it on your hard drive.

PC WITH WINDOWS 95 OR 98

The program should start automatically when you put the disk in the CD drive. If it does not, follow these instructions.

❶ Put the disk in the CD drive
❷ Open MY COMPUTER
❸ Double-click on the CD drive icon
❹ Double-click on the icon called SOLAR

PC WITH WINDOWS 3.1 OR 3.11

❶ Put the disk in the CD drive
❷ Select RUN from the FILE menu in the PROGRAM MANAGER
❸ Type D:\SOLAR (Where D is the letter of your CD drive)
❹ Press the RETURN key

APPLE MACINTOSH

❶ Put the disk in the CD drive
❷ Double click on the INTERFACT icon
❸ Double click on the icon called SOLAR

CHECKLIST

● Firstly, make sure that your computer and monitor meet the system requirements as set out on page 40.

● Ensure that your computer, monitor and CD-ROM drive are all switched on and working normally.

● It is important that you do not have any other applications, such as wordprocessors, running. Before starting INTERFACT quit all other applications.

● Make sure that any screen savers have been switched off.

● If you are running INTERFACT on a PC with Windows 3.1 or 3.11, make sure that you type in the correct instructions when loading the disk, using a colon (:) not a semi-colon (;) and a back slash (\) not a forward slash (/). Also, do not use any other punctuation or put any spaces between letters.

How to use INTERFACT

INTERFACT is easy to use.
First find out how to load the program
(see page 40), then read these simple
instructions and dive in!

You will find that there are lots of different features to explore.
To select one, operate the controls on the right-hand side of the screen. You will see that the main area of the screen changes as you click on different features.

For example, this is what your screen will look like when you play Rocket Mission, a journey of discovery through the solar system. Once you've selected a feature, click on the main screen to start playing.

You have arrived at Jupiter.

Click to continue.

Click here to select the feature you want to play.

Click on the arrow keys to scroll through the different features on the disk or find your way to the exit.

This is the text box, where instructions and directions appear. See page 4 to find out what's on the disk.

DISK LINKS

When you read the book, you'll come across Disk Links. These show you where to find activities on the disk that relate to the page you are reading. Use the arrow keys to find the icon on screen that matches the one in the Disk Link.

DISK LINK
Save Alan the Astronaut by getting your space facts right when you play Lost in Space!

BOOKMARKS

As you explore the features on the disk, you'll bump into Bookmarks. These show you where to look in the book for more information about the topic on screen. Just turn to the page of the book shown in the Bookmark.

23

LAB PAGES

On pages 36–39, you'll find grid pages to photocopy. These are for making notes and recording any thoughts or ideas you may have as you read the book.

HOT DISK TIPS

• After you have chosen the feature you want to play, remember to move the cursor from the icon to the main screen before clicking the mouse again.

• If you don't know how to use one of the on-screen controls, simply touch it with your cursor. An explanation will pop up in the text box!

• Keep a close eye on the cursor. When it changes from an arrow ➡ to a hand, ☞ click your mouse and something will happen.

• Any words that appear on screen in blue and underlined are "hot." This means you can touch them with the cursor for more information.

• Explore the screen! There are secret hot spots and hidden surprises to find.

Troubleshooting

If you come across a problem loading or running the INTERFACT disk, you should find the solution here. If you still cannot solve your problem, call the helpline at 1-609-921-6700

QUICK FIXES Run through these general checkpoints before consulting COMMON PROBLEMS (see opposite page).

QUICK FIXES **PC WITH WINDOWS 3.1 OR 3.11**

1 Check that you have the minimum system requirements: 386/33Mhz, VGA color monitor, 4Mb of RAM.

2 Make sure you have typed in the correct instructions: a colon (:) not a semi-colon (;) and a back slash (\) not a forward slash (/). Also, do not put any spaces between letters or punctuation.

3 It is important that you do not have any other programs running. Before you start **INTERFACT**, hold down the Control key and press Escape. If you find that other programs are open, click on them with the mouse, then click the End Task key.

QUICK FIXES **PC WITH WINDOWS 95**

1 Make sure you have typed in the correct instructions: a colon (:) not a semi-colon (;) and a back slash(\) not a forward slash (/). Also, do not put any spaces between letters or punctuation.

2 It is important that you do not have any other programs running. Before you start **INTERFACT**, look at the task bar. If you find that other programs are open, click with the right mouse button and select Close from the pop-up menu.

MACINTOSH

1 Make sure that you have the minimum system requirements: 68020 processor, 640x480 color display, system 7.0 (or a later version), and 4Mb of RAM.

2 It is important that you do not have any other programs running. Before you start **INTERFACT**, click on the application menu in the top right-hand corner. Select each of the open applications and select Quit from the File menu.

COMMON PROBLEMS

Symptom: Cannot load disk.
Problem: There is not enough space available on your hard disk
Solution: Make more space available by deleting old applications and files you don't use until 6Mb of free space is available.

Symptom: Disk will not run.
Problem: There is not enough memory available.
Solution: *Either* quit other open applications (see Quick Fixes) *or* increase your machine's RAM by adjusting the Virtual Memory.

Symptom: Graphics do not load or are poor quality.
Problem: *Either* there is not enough memory available *or* you have the wrong display setting.
Solution: *Either* quit other applications (see Quick Fixes) *or* make sure that your monitor control is set to 640x480x256 or VGA.

Symptom: There is no sound (PCs only).
Problem: Your sound card is not Soundblaster compatible.
Solution: Try to configure your sound settings to make them Soundblaster compatible (refer to your sound card manual for more details).

Symptom: Your machine freezes.
Problem: There is not enough memory available.
Solution: *Either* quit other applications (see Quick Fixes) *or* increase your machine's RAM by adjusting the Virtual Memory.

Symptom: Text does not fit neatly into boxes and "hot" copy does not bring up extra information.
Problem: Standard fonts on your computer have been moved or deleted.
Solution: Reinstall standard fonts. The PC version requires Arial; the Macintosh version requires Helvetica. See your computer manual for further information.

Index

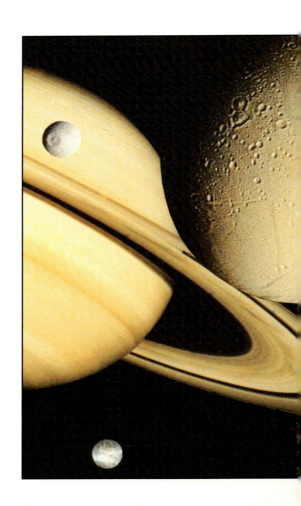